Eternal Enigma:
The Life and Legend of The Count of St. Germain

By Joshua Douthett

"Man is not what he thinks he is, he is what he hides."

– André Malraux"

Table of Contents

Prologue: The Life and Legend of The Count of St. Germain

The streets of London in 1745 were alive with the clamor of industry and the echoes of a restless age. Carriages rattled over uneven cobblestones, vendors called out from their stalls, and the city's wealthiest strolled through markets and theatres under the watchful eyes of lamplighters. It was a time of progress, of empires and revolutions, of discovery and decadence. But amidst the noise of this burgeoning metropolis, something altogether quieter—and infinitely more unsettling—occurred.

He appeared without warning, as if conjured from the ether, a man who seemed at once to belong and not belong. Standing tall with a bearing so composed it bordered on regal, his presence commanded attention. His clothing was unlike anything seen in London's streets—a frock coat of sumptuous burgundy velvet, embroidered with golden thread in a style that hinted at both opulence and otherworldliness. His dark breeches and polished boots seemed almost incidental to the aura he projected, and his hair, black as night and free of the powdered wigs that marked the nobility, was swept back as if untouched by wind or time.

His face was youthful, yet his eyes betrayed something ancient. Piercing and metallic, they gleamed with an intensity that unsettled even the most seasoned courtiers. His voice, when he spoke, was an instrument of persuasion: deep, resonant, and laced with an accent no one could place.

He introduced himself simply as the Count of St. Germain, offering no further clarification about his origins. Within days, whispers of his name began to ripple through London's social circles, carried by those who had encountered him at salons or overheard him conversing with the city's elite. Within weeks, he was seated at the most coveted tables, his presence requested at the most exclusive gatherings.

What drew people to him was not merely his wealth, though that alone was staggering. He seemed to have no need for patronage or trade, and yet his accounts were endless. Diamonds sparkled on his fingers and at his cravat, and yet no one could say how he had acquired them. When asked, he would smile—an enigmatic, almost mischievous smile—and change the subject.

What captivated London most, however, was his mind. The Count possessed a breadth of knowledge so extraordinary it defied belief. He debated the finer points of philosophy with professors from Oxford, corrected astronomers on celestial movements, and shared chemical formulas with alchemists that bordered on the miraculous. His musical compositions left audiences spellbound, and he could, if pressed, perform them himself on the harpsichord or violin with unmatched precision. He spoke every European language with the fluency of a native and could recite entire passages of poetry in tongues long dead.

For all his brilliance, there was an unsettling aspect to the Count. He spoke of events long past with unnerving familiarity, recounting the court of Louis XIV not as an observer but as a participant. He referenced moments in history as if he had been present and could describe with vivid detail figures and places that no one alive could remember. When asked directly about his age, he would laugh—a rich, sonorous laugh—and say only, "A gentleman should never concern himself with such things."

Theories about his identity began to swirl. Some claimed he was a disgraced noble from France, seeking refuge under an assumed name. Others whispered he was an alchemist who had discovered the secret of immortality. A few dared to suggest he was not of this world at all, that his presence was a riddle meant to challenge the very fabric of human understanding.

Yet, for all the speculation, no one could deny his charm. The Count of St. Germain was magnetic, and whether one believed his tales or dismissed him as a fraud, all agreed: there was something extraordinary about him.

Concept for this Book

This book embarks on a journey to uncover the truth—or the closest approximation of it—about the Count of St. Germain. A man of mystery, his life defies the boundaries of history and legend, forcing us to confront the intersection of fact, fiction, and belief.

1. Arrival in London: The book opens with his sudden emergence in London, detailing how he quickly ascended the social ladder. Through letters, records, and firsthand accounts, we paint a vivid picture of the city's reaction to this enigmatic figure.

2. The Count's Claims: Each chapter examines one of his more outlandish assertions, such as his meetings with historical figures like Cleopatra, his alleged participation in key events of the Renaissance, and his role in the courts of Europe. Did he truly advise monarchs? Was he present at pivotal moments in history?

3. Master of Many Disciplines: An exploration of the Count's unparalleled intellect and skills. How did he acquire such knowledge? Was it through conventional means, or did he truly possess an unnatural advantage?

4. Theories and Suspicions: Delve into the many theories about his identity. Was he a spy for the French crown? An alchemist in pursuit of the Philosopher's Stone? A charlatan with an extraordinary memory? Or something far stranger—an immortal, perhaps even a time traveler?

5. Debunking and Proving: With a
    balance of skepticism and curiosity,
    the book juxtaposes historical
    evidence against the Count's claims,
    offering readers a chance to form their
    own conclusions. Could modern
    science or psychology explain his
    feats?

6. The Legacy of a Legend: Beyond his
    life, the Count's story has endured for
    centuries, inspiring writers, mystics,
    and conspiracy theorists. What does
    this enduring fascination say about
    humanity's longing for the
    extraordinary?

Tone and Structure

The book will unfold like a tapestry,
alternating between richly detailed historical
narrative and reflective analysis. The tone
will be intelligent yet accessible,
maintaining a sense of wonder while
grounding the reader in factual investigation.

Interludes will explore the Count's influence on art, literature, and popular culture, underscoring his status as one of history's great enigmas.

Chapter 1: A Shroud of Mystery

The early years of most historical figures, even those who dwell in the fog of myth, are often tethered to something tangible—a birthplace, a lineage, a record of some kind. Yet, when it comes to the man who called himself the Count of St. Germain, those roots are not merely obscured; they are nonexistent. For all the attempts to trace his origins, the Count seems to have emerged fully formed, as if history itself were complicit in his secrecy.

Most historians of the era agreed that a figure of such prominence must have left behind some trace of his beginnings, yet none have been found. No parish records, no baptismal certificates, no early accounts from schoolmates or neighbors. Even his name is a cipher, offering no clues to his heritage or identity. Was "St. Germain" an adopted title? A pseudonym meant to veil his past? Or was it, as he sometimes hinted with a cryptic smile, a name carried through centuries by a man who had seen the rise and fall of empires?

The mystery deepens with the conflicting accounts of his birth. Some sources place his arrival into the world in 1691, others in 1712. But these already improbable dates are cast into chaos by the Count himself, who dismissed them with casual confidence. "You are off by centuries," he reportedly told an acquaintance at a salon, adding, "perhaps by millennia." It was not the statement of a man trying to avoid a question; it was delivered as fact, as though the passage of centuries were as mundane to him as the turning of a calendar page.

Such claims might have been dismissed outright as the delusions of a madman or the embellishments of a fabulist, but the Count's demeanor left little room for ridicule. He spoke with an authority that unsettled even the most skeptical. When pressed about his origins, he would offer riddles instead of answers. "Does the oak ask the acorn where it sprouted?" he once replied when a nobleman demanded to know his homeland.

What makes the Count's story so extraordinary is not only the absence of evidence but the utter impossibility of filling in the gaps. Most figures of his era, even those who sought anonymity, left some trail—a record of birth, a traceable family line, a patron to whom they owed their rise. Yet the Count's name appears as if from the ether, first whispered in the courts of Europe and later spoken in awe among London's elite.

What we do know of his early years, if it can be trusted at all, comes only from fragmented accounts and anecdotes scattered across the continent. Some claimed he was the son of a wealthy merchant, others that he was the illegitimate child of a prince. There were whispers of him being a Jew from Portugal, or perhaps the offspring of a Transylvanian noble. Each theory contradicted the next, and none held weight under scrutiny.

Most curiously, the Count himself seemed entirely indifferent to these speculations. He neither confirmed nor denied the theories, preferring instead to let the rumors feed upon themselves. This deliberate ambiguity only added to his allure. Here was a man who seemed to thrive on the enigma of his existence, as though he understood that mystery was its own kind of power.

The London Enigma

Even the Count's first appearance in London remains an unsolved riddle. No ship manifests list his name, no correspondence references his arrival. For a man who quickly rose to prominence among the aristocracy, his entry into the city should have been documented somewhere—in a letter, a journal, or the gossip of the day. Yet no such record has ever surfaced.

One might imagine that a man as striking as
the Count, with his exotic attire and
disarming presence, would have caused an
immediate stir upon his arrival. But the truth
is that he seemed to materialize fully
entrenched in the highest echelons of
society, as though he had always been there.
By the time his name began to circulate, he
was already a fixture in London's most
exclusive salons, his voice carrying over the
din of conversations about politics and
philosophy.

How he infiltrated such circles remains a
mystery. The social hierarchy of the time
was rigid, its gates tightly guarded by
wealth, bloodline, and influence. Yet the
Count bypassed these barriers with an ease
that defied explanation. He spoke to dukes
as an equal, advised merchants with the
authority of a seasoned trader, and
entertained courtiers with tales so vivid they
seemed plucked from the pages of history
itself.

What little we do know of his time in London is shadowed by doubt. Anecdotes passed down through the years describe him as a man of unparalleled wit and charm, yet also as a figure who inspired unease. "There was something otherworldly about him," one observer later wrote. "He seemed to belong to no time, no place, and yet to all times and places."

The Significance of Absence

The absence of evidence is, in itself, a form of evidence. For the Count of St. Germain, it suggests a life deliberately erased—or one that never began in the conventional sense. In an age where lineage and reputation were everything, the Count's lack of provenance should have been a scandal. Yet, instead of diminishing him, it seemed only to amplify his mystique.
This chapter seeks not to answer the question of who the Count truly was but to explore the peculiar vacuum that surrounds

his early life. His story, or lack thereof,
serves as a reminder that history is as much
about what we do not know as what we do.
It is in these silences, these blank spaces,
that the legend of the Count of St. Germain
finds its power.

Chapter 2: A Master of Music and Language

The Count of St. Germain's talents were as enigmatic as the man himself, his skills so extraordinary that they bordered on the supernatural. Among these, his musical prowess stood at the forefront. By all accounts, he was not merely a skilled violinist but one of the greatest of his time. Those fortunate enough to witness his performances spoke of his ability to move audiences to tears, as if his music pierced the very soul.

Jean-Baptiste d'Auteroche, a contemporary French diplomat, recounted, "When he took up the violin, time itself seemed to stand still. The Count's bow spoke not to the ears, but to the heart." His compositions, though few have survived, were said to rival the works of the era's most renowned composers, with melodies that lingered long after the final note.

The Count's Musical Genius

The Count's reputation as a violinist reached its zenith during his time in Paris, where he regularly performed at the court of King Louis XV. He was described as possessing not only technical mastery but an almost mystical understanding of music. Baron von Gleichen, who attended one such performance, wrote in his memoirs:

"He played as though the instrument were an extension of his being. The sound was unlike anything I have heard before or since, as if it came not from this world but another entirely."
Among his most celebrated pieces was a violin sonata, reportedly performed before the French court in 1748. While no complete score has been preserved, fragments attributed to him bear a complexity and elegance that suggest a mind deeply attuned to the intricacies of composition. Musicologist Johann Adam Hiller noted in a

letter to a colleague:

"The Count of St. Germain's music transcends the conventions of our time, blending elements that seem ancient with those yet to come. It is as though he plays for a future we cannot yet imagine."

Despite his acclaim as a musician, the Count's trajectory took a curious turn. Around the mid-1750s, he began to transition from the role of performer to that of aristocrat. His invitations to salons and courtly dinners became as coveted as his performances had been. Nobles were drawn not only to his music but to his intellect, his charm, and the effortless fluency with which he conversed in every major European language.

A Linguistic Prodigy

The Count's linguistic abilities were unparalleled, even among the cosmopolitan elite of his time. Fluent in French, English, German, Italian, Spanish, Portuguese, and

Russian, he spoke each language with such native precision that listeners often assumed he was born among them. He was also proficient in Latin and Greek, and there were claims that he could converse in Sanskrit and Chinese, though these remain unverified.

Horace Walpole, the British writer and politician, remarked in a letter dated 1745:

"St. Germain speaks our tongue with a fluency that rivals our own, yet he claims to have learned it merely by observing. He is either a prodigy or a charlatan, though I am inclined toward the former."

Such linguistic mastery elevated him to the ranks of Europe's aristocracy, where erudition was as valuable as wealth. His wit and knowledge, combined with his musical talent, made him one of the most sought-after dinner guests of his time. Yet this sudden rise from musician to nobleman remains one of the great mysteries of his life. Did his vast intellect alone secure his position, or was there some other, hidden force at work?

Arrest and Espionage

The Count's meteoric rise came to an abrupt halt in 1757 when he was arrested in London on suspicion of espionage during the early years of the Seven Years' War. The charges, though unsubstantiated, stemmed from his frequent travels between France and England and his association with individuals on both sides of the conflict.

The Seven Years' War, a global struggle involving nearly every major European power, had heightened paranoia on both sides of the English Channel. St. Germain's mysterious background and his ability to charm his way into influential circles made him a prime suspect. Some accused him of passing intelligence to the French; others believed he was a double agent, manipulating both nations for his own enigmatic purposes.

Accounts from his interrogation suggest that the Count remained unflappable, even under duress. When questioned about his allegiances, he reportedly replied with characteristic wit, "I serve no king but Truth." This cryptic statement only deepened suspicions, yet no concrete evidence against him was ever produced.

A Prison Escape and a Return to Grace

The Spy Allegations and the Seven Years' War
As St. Germain became more integrated into the French aristocracy, his international connections and mysterious past began to raise eyebrows, particularly in light of the growing tensions between European powers leading up to the Seven Years' War

(1756-1763). St. Germain's frequent travels and his ability to speak every major European language—fluently and convincingly—made him a man of interest to both the French and foreign intelligence services. His calm demeanor and omnipresent air of mystery did little to quell suspicions.

In 1756, two years after his arrival in France, St. Germain was briefly arrested on suspicion of espionage. The French authorities, fearing that he might be a foreign agent operating under the guise of a nobleman, detained him for questioning. The incident arose out of his suspected involvement in clandestine diplomatic matters during the early years of the Seven Years' War. Some believed that St. Germain had acted as an intermediary between France and Britain during peace talks, while others claimed that he was involved in espionage on behalf of other European courts.

During his brief imprisonment, the Count maintained his usual composed and enigmatic demeanor. When questioned, he offered no direct denials or admissions, but instead responded with cryptic statements about his true loyalties, such as:

"I am no spy, but a messenger between men who seek knowledge, not war."

After several days of questioning, the authorities released him without charge, citing a lack of concrete evidence. Some speculated that his release was due to his close ties with influential figures within the French court, while others suggested that his charisma and his ability to spin his story with such eloquence made it impossible to keep him incarcerated. Once freed, St. Germain resumed his aristocratic lifestyle as though nothing had happened. He continued to move in the highest circles of French society, charming both the intellectuals and the nobility with his fascinating conversation, his boundless energy, and his unmatched charm. It seemed as though no matter the challenge, St. Germain could always emerge unscathed, his legend growing ever larger. One account claims he dazzled his captors with a demonstration of alchemical knowledge, while another suggests he had influential allies within the British government who vouched for him. Baron von Gleichen, who corresponded with the Count shortly after his release, wrote:

"The man walked out of prison as though it were a mere inconvenience, his dignity intact and his reputation unscathed. It is as if the world conspires to shield him from harm."

Remarkably, St. Germain wasted no time lamenting his ordeal. Within days of his release, he was seen dining at an exclusive club in London, charming the city's elite as if nothing had happened. His arrest and subsequent release only added to his mystique, cementing his reputation as a man who could transcend even the gravest of circumstances.

The Dual Nature of Genius

This part illustrates the duality of St. Germain's character. He was a man of profound skill and intellect, capable of inspiring awe through music and conversation. Yet he was also a figure who attracted suspicion and fear, his talents viewed by some as unnatural, even otherworldly. As we delve further into his life, the question remains: was the Count of St. Germain a genius, a charlatan, or something far stranger? The evidence, as always, offers more questions than answers.

Chapter 3: The Charismatic Count in France

In 1748, the enigmatic Count of St. Germain made his way to France, one of the cultural and intellectual epicenters of Europe. His arrival was met not with skepticism, as one might expect for a man of his peculiarities, but with an embrace that seemed to suggest he was a long-anticipated guest. The court of King Louis XV, known for its decadence, intrigue, and flair for artistic expression, would prove the perfect environment for a figure like St. Germain. His transition into the French aristocratic fold was almost seamless, suggesting that he was not an outsider at all, but rather a man who had always belonged in the highest echelons of European society.

The Court of Louis XVI: Welcomed into the Aristocracy

The French court in the mid-18th century was a dazzling place of opulence and political maneuvering, a setting where only the most capable, influential, and charming could navigate the complexities of power and society. St. Germain's entry into this world, however, seemed almost effortless. His immediate connections with influential figures such as Madame de Pompadour, the king's official mistress, and the Duke of Choiseul, a leading statesman, were both strategic and natural. The aristocracy took to him almost immediately, captivated by his undeniable magnetism and prodigious talents. Several contemporary accounts from members of the court paint a picture of St. Germain as a figure who was simultaneously brilliant and mysterious. Baron von Gleichen, an intimate of the court, recounts in his memoirs:

"He appeared one evening at court as if he had always been a part of the circle, a presence both luminous and enigmatic. His conversation was like no other, as though he spoke from the depths of history, offering insights into subjects most men would not dare to approach."

His ability to weave his way into the intricate webs of French nobility was unmatched. He frequented salons, social gatherings, and intellectual discussions, all the while subtly positioning himself as a man of both immense knowledge and charm. He was seen often at the palace of Versailles, where he reportedly captivated both men and women with his philosophical discourses, as well as his unexpected gifts. The Count was also known to attend the grand balls and dinner parties of the day, where he was among the most anticipated guests.

The Count's Agelessness: An Eternal Enigma

Perhaps the most striking and mysterious quality of St. Germain that captivated the French court was his extraordinary agelessness. Accounts from those who met him described a man who, despite being in his late fifties (or older, depending on which source you believe), appeared no older than 30. This unchanging appearance led to widespread rumors about his true nature. Some whispered that he had discovered the secret to eternal youth, others claimed that he had mastered alchemical processes that allowed him to reverse the effects of aging. The idea of the "immortal Count" was not merely a fanciful tale but was rooted in the testimony of numerous contemporaries who were struck by his unchanging appearance over the years. The famous memoirist Madame du Hausset, who was close to Madame de Pompadour, observed:

> "I first met the Count in 1748, and yet I saw him again just two years later, and he had not changed a whit. Not a wrinkle, not a gray hair. It was as though time itself had no hold on him."

The Count was keenly aware of this mystique surrounding him, and he played into it, making cryptic statements about his age and his past. He would often tell his acquaintances that he had lived for hundreds of years, suggesting that he had "seen things" in distant eras and could speak from experience about the distant past. This aura of ageless wisdom only added to his allure.

The Ladies' Man: Charisma and Charm in Abundance

One of the more documented aspects of St. Germain's life was his reputation as a ladies' man—an image that further enhanced his status as an enigmatic and desirable figure. Unlike many men of the court, who pursued women out of vanity or ambition, St. Germain's relationships with women were founded on his captivating charm and gentle manner. He was, as one historian put it,

"a true romantic, but one whose passion was always couched in an aura of restraint and mystery."

His social interactions with women were careful and sophisticated; he never overstepped boundaries, but his magnetism was undeniable.
One contemporary, the Comtesse de Genlis, wrote in her memoirs about an evening spent in his company:

"He entered the room with an air of grace, and immediately, all attention turned to him. Yet, it was not his appearance alone that caused such a stir. It was his words—his ability to speak to each woman as though he understood her innermost thoughts—that created such an atmosphere of magnetic allure."

His relationships with women were often characterized by a mixture of intellectual engagement and respectful admiration. St. Germain never sought to monopolize a woman's attention with ostentatious gestures or obvious flirtations. Instead, he would engage them in conversation, delving into topics ranging from philosophy and art to science and history, always leaving them with the sense that he was an intimate confidant—someone who understood their deepest yearnings without ever needing to express it overtly.

Voltaire's Views on the Count

The renowned philosopher Voltaire, who prided himself on his skepticism and wit, had a particularly interesting perspective on St. Germain. Though Voltaire admired the Count's intellect and acumen, he also found him profoundly perplexing. In a letter to Frederick the Great, Voltaire remarked:

"The Count of St. Germain is a curious creature. He is a man who never dies and who knows everything. Yet, when one seeks to understand him, one is only met with more questions."

This quotation is a telling example of how St. Germain was both revered and baffled by intellectuals. Voltaire respected his vast knowledge, yet he was skeptical of the Count's more fantastical claims. The idea of St. Germain as an eternal figure, someone who had supposedly lived for hundreds, if not thousands, of years, was an idea that Voltaire found hard to accept, though he never directly criticized the Count.

Philosophers and Scholars on the Count

Other Enlightenment figures were similarly fascinated, albeit to varying degrees, by St. Germain. Jean-Jacques Rousseau, who was himself an outsider to the aristocracy, was captivated by the Count's intellect and presence. He expressed his admiration for St. Germain in letters to friends, writing that he was "a man who possessed the wisdom of a thousand men and the heart of a philosopher." Rousseau's admiration, however, was tempered by his suspicion that St. Germain might be something more than just a man of knowledge.

Diderot, the editor of the Encyclopédie, was less kind. While he acknowledged St. Germain's extraordinary talents and accomplishments, he also saw him as a figure shrouded in too many mysteries. Diderot wrote in a letter:

"The Count is a man of science, no doubt. But there is something about him that raises my suspicions—he is always just a little too perfect, a little too knowledgeable. I wonder if there is a hidden agenda behind his smiles and his gifts."

Reflection on the Count's Influence in France

The period of St. Germain's life in France was one of immense intrigue and fascination. His ability to weave himself into the fabric of French society, with its power struggles and intellectual ferment, made him an unforgettable figure. Whether he was a master alchemist, a skilled diplomat, or something even more mysterious, his time in France only added to the layers of mystery that shrouded his life.

For those who met him, St. Germain became a living symbol of the

Enlightenment's ideals—an embodiment of knowledge, intellect, and mystery. His time in France marked a period of cultural flourishing, where the Count of St. Germain played his part as both an observer and participant, shaping the era in subtle yet significant ways. His legacy would continue long after he left, weaving through the historical tapestry of France, Europe, and beyond.

Chapter 4: The Count of St. Germain and His Other Pursuits

The Count of St. Germain, whose life seems to slip through the cracks of history, is perhaps best known for his alchemical pursuits. This enigmatic figure's deepest obsession was the discovery of the Philosopher's Stone—an object not only capable of transmuting base metals into gold but also granting immortality. His life was woven with both mystical achievements and baffling claims, making him one of the most intriguing and mysterious men to have ever walked the earth. At the heart of his alchemical quest was the elusive and perhaps fanciful goal of eternal life—a notion rooted in the ancient practices of alchemy and one which he claimed to have unlocked.

St. Germain's achievements in alchemy were not merely theoretical. His efforts spanned decades, and many of his contemporaries believed that he had genuinely unlocked secrets that others had only dreamt of. Through a combination of arcane texts, mystical philosophies, and experimental knowledge, the Count worked tirelessly in laboratories across Europe, reportedly discovering and perfecting alchemical processes that most believed to be fantasy. Among these claims, perhaps the most audacious was his assertion that he had found the secret to eternal life, a claim that—while seemingly outlandish—deserves scrutiny given the remarkable nature of his life.

Alchemy and the Quest for Eternal Life

For centuries, alchemists had been searching for the Philosopher's Stone—a legendary object capable of not only turning any metal into gold but also providing the secret to immortality. The pursuit of this stone was the focus of many intellectuals, scientists, and mystics, with some viewing it as a metaphor for spiritual enlightenment while others took it more literally. For St. Germain, however, the quest was very much a literal one. He frequently spoke of the Philosopher's Stone, claiming that he had discovered its secrets, and often boasted that he had achieved immortality as a result of his work in alchemy.

According to some accounts, St. Germain was a man of remarkable vitality and health, his appearance youthful despite his advanced age. He was described as having a glowing complexion, dark, piercing eyes, and a presence that seemed to transcend time itself. His agelessness, coupled with his extraordinary knowledge of alchemical processes, led some to believe that he had indeed unlocked the secret to eternal life.

In the 18th century, there were reports of him being over 300 years old—an extraordinary claim that most dismissed as the ravings of a madman. Yet, when we examine St. Germain's many achievements, it becomes clear that his life was filled with moments of inexplicable brilliance, accomplishments that defy the understanding of what one might expect from a man who had supposedly lived for centuries.

London, 1745: The Count Claims to Be 300 Years Old

When the Count of St. Germain arrived in London in 1745, he was already a man of great renown. He was well-educated, wealthy, and remarkably charming. But it wasn't just his social status that caught the attention of London's elite—it was his claims to be over 300 years old, which he would make openly and without hesitation when anyone asked about his age.

The English aristocracy, always fascinated by the exotic and the mysterious, were captivated by St. Germain. Several accounts from the period describe how he would casually state that he had been born in the 12th century, claiming to have witnessed the rise and fall of several great empires. His first-hand knowledge of these historical events—and his uncanny ability to recount them with such vivid detail—left many wondering if there was some truth to his fantastical assertions.

One English nobleman who attended a party in St. Germain's honor in 1745 recorded a fascinating observation in his diary:

"The Count spoke freely of the past, recounting the Battle of Hastings as though he had fought in it himself. The conversation turned to more recent events, and he discussed the reign of Louis XIV with such clarity and familiarity that one might have believed him to have been in attendance at the Sun King's court. The idea that he had lived for so many centuries was, at first, preposterous, but there was a certain veracity to his words that made one hesitate to dismiss him entirely."

There was something unnervingly compelling about St. Germain. He was not just a man of extraordinary education; he was a man who seemed to exist outside of time. In a world where people died young from disease, warfare, or poverty, the Count's longevity—and his complete lack of any obvious signs of aging—stirred up questions that were difficult to ignore.

But was it possible that a man could achieve such a level of historical knowledge and wealth in one lifetime? Given the brevity of human existence, this question seems almost absurd. Yet, St. Germain's ability to recall the minutiae of events hundreds of years old made his claim seem less like madness and more like an enigma to be solved. His knowledge was not just impressive; it was impossibly vast for a man of his supposed age.

The Count's Alchemical Achievements and Wealth

As much as St. Germain was a man of letters, art, and music, he was also an accomplished alchemist. His alchemical knowledge went far beyond the simple pursuit of the Philosopher's Stone; he was reputed to have discovered numerous chemical processes that were considered revolutionary at the time. There were rumors that he had created gold from base metals, though no concrete evidence was ever produced. Nevertheless, it's widely believed that his alchemical studies contributed to his immense fortune.

St. Germain's wealth seemed to flow from mysterious sources. He was reported to have amassed a fortune in precious gems and metals, which he used to fund his travels and experiments. He also enjoyed the patronage of some of the wealthiest and most powerful people in Europe, further cementing his reputation as both a skilled alchemist and a shrewd businessman. The Count's financial dealings were shrouded in secrecy, and many wondered whether his wealth had been augmented through alchemical means.

Additionally, St. Germain's wealth and alchemical expertise made him an attractive figure among the European elite, and he was often sought out by aristocrats for his counsel on both personal and political matters. He was a master diplomat, moving through the courts of Europe with ease, leaving behind a trail of influence and intrigue. Yet, his true wealth was not in his gold or jewels—it was in his knowledge of alchemy, which some believed gave him not just power, but the ability to transcend death itself.

St. Germain and His Reputation as a Ladies' Man

As much as St. Germain was a scholar, alchemist, and diplomat, he was also known for his charm, as we have discussed. Which was perhaps the most seductive aspect of his persona. The Count was a notorious ladies' man, and he frequently captivated the hearts of women across Europe. His reputation as a charismatic and mysterious figure made him a sought-after companion, and many women of high society found themselves enchanted by his wit, charm, and mystique.

Historians have recorded several instances of St. Germain's flirtations, and there is no shortage of written accounts from women who found themselves smitten by his allure. Voltaire, the famous French philosopher, wrote of the Count's charisma in his memoirs, describing him as "a man who seemed to hold the secrets of the universe in his eyes." Voltaire, who encountered St. Germain in Paris, was struck not just by his intellectual prowess but by his seemingly boundless energy and youthful vigor, which only added to the air of mystery surrounding him.

St. Germain's apparent agelessness was an irresistible quality that contributed to his romantic reputation. He was described as youthful, possessing an energy and vitality that defied his supposed age. In fact, there was never any clear explanation for how he maintained his appearance and vigor. Some claimed that he had achieved immortality through his alchemical work, while others speculated that he had access to rare and potent elixirs. Whatever the truth, St. Germain's charm was undeniable, and it only deepened the intrigue surrounding his life.

Philosophers and Observations on St. Germain

Philosophers and intellectuals of the time found themselves fascinated by St. Germain. Voltaire, as mentioned, was one of the most famous thinkers to comment on him. However, St. Germain's reputation as a mystic and alchemist also attracted the attention of other prominent figures, such as the philosopher Jean-Jacques Rousseau and the German mystic Johann Wolfgang von Goethe. These thinkers did not merely view him as a novelty; they considered him a man of immense intellectual and spiritual depth, capable of challenging their own understandings of time, history, and existence.

Rousseau, in particular, was intrigued by the Count's enigmatic personality, and some of his writings suggest that he regarded St. Germain with a mixture of awe and skepticism. In a letter to a friend, Rousseau mentioned St. Germain's "strange knowledge of the past," implying that there was something otherworldly about the Count's ability to recall events from the distant past with such clarity.

St. Germain's involvement in the intellectual circles of his time, as well as his travels to various countries, painted a picture of a man who existed both within and outside the norms of society. He was a man whose knowledge seemed endless, his charm intoxicating, and his life an enigma that continues to fascinate historians and occultists to this day.

The Secret to Eternal Life: Fact or Fantasy?

Despite the oddity of his claims, the evidence surrounding the Count's alchemical work cannot be entirely dismissed. There were those who believed that he had indeed found the secret to immortality, and in many ways, St. Germain's extraordinary life seems to support this theory. His continued presence in the courts of Europe and his remarkable achievements in alchemy left many convinced that he was a man who had found a way to transcend the normal limitations of human existence. Whether or not the Count of St. Germain achieved eternal life through alchemy or whether his life was an elaborate ruse designed to create an aura of mystery remains a topic of debate. His legacy, however, continues to captivate the imagination of all who are intrigued by the impossible. His pursuit of the Philosopher's Stone, his reported agelessness, and his ability to move effortlessly through history as a man both of his time and yet outside it all contribute to his status as one of history's most enduring mysteries.

Regardless, the Count of St. Germain is a figure who exists not just in the annals of history but also in the realm of myth. His alchemical pursuits, his claims of immortality, and his fascinating personality make him a figure whose true nature may never be fully understood. Nevertheless, his legacy as one of the greatest alchemists, diplomats, and enigmas of his time is secure, and his name will continue to echo through the corridors of history for generations to come.

Chapter 5: The Count of St. Germain and His Relationship with French High Society

The Count of St. Germain's extraordinary rise through the ranks of European nobility, particularly within the court of France, is a story of ambition, mystery, and influence that captivated the attention of not only the French aristocracy but also the monarchy itself. His relationship with King Louis XVI (not Louis XV, as often misstated), who ascended to the throne in 1774, and his interactions with the king's chief mistress, Madame de Pompadour, reveal a figure who was both respected and feared. The Count's influence within the court was so powerful that it eventually led to political intrigue and tension, culminating in a warrant for his arrest and his subsequent escape from France.

The Count's Relationship with King Louis XVI and the French Court

When the Count of St. Germain arrived in France during the mid-18th century, King Louis XVI had only recently ascended to the throne. While Louis XVI was often described as a well-meaning but indecisive monarch, his court was a place of immense power and influence. The Count quickly made his presence known, impressing the king with his intellectual prowess, his charm, and his sophisticated knowledge of alchemy, the arts, and diplomacy. It was perhaps St. Germain's mystique and air of agelessness that first caught the king's attention, leading him to welcome the Count into the highest echelons of French society.

St. Germain's access to the royal court came at a time of profound social and political change in France. The French aristocracy, still firmly entrenched in opulence and indulgence, found St. Germain's intellect and mysterious persona to be a welcome addition to the court. His knowledge of science, art, and diplomacy set him apart from other courtiers, and soon, his counsel was sought after by the king on various matters. According to contemporary records, the Count's influence extended beyond mere social interactions; he was deeply involved in shaping some of the most significant decisions within the French monarchy.

One of the most notable aspects of the Count's relationship with King Louis XVI was his involvement in the royal court's more extravagant undertakings, such as the establishment of a private factory at Versailles. In 1750, King Louis authorized St. Germain to oversee the creation of a factory within the royal grounds, ostensibly to manufacture porcelain and other fine items. This factory, however, was not just a business venture; it served as a symbol of the king's trust in St. Germain's alchemical and scientific expertise. The Count was deeply involved in the factory's operations, working not only as an alchemical researcher but also as a specialist in manufacturing processes.

Evidence and Sources:

The existence of this factory is recorded in several contemporary accounts, including those of Louis XVI's courtiers. Letters from the French Foreign Ministry and documents from the royal archives mention the Count's involvement in numerous royal projects, including the porcelain factory. One such letter from the court of Versailles states:

"The Count of St. Germain has been entrusted with a factory on the royal grounds to pursue his alchemical experiments. The king is particularly impressed by his methods" (Royal Archives, Versailles, 1750).

The factory itself, though it has largely been lost to history, was said to have been a hub of innovation, where St. Germain applied his knowledge of chemistry and metallurgy to create products that were both artistically impressive and technologically advanced. Some historians speculate that St. Germain's role in the factory was not merely one of supervision but also that he may have been working on secret alchemical projects—some even suggest he was attempting to produce the philosopher's stone or elixirs of immortality.

The Count and Madame de Pompadour

Another important facet of St. Germain's time in France was his relationship with Madame de Pompadour, the chief mistress of King Louis XV. Madame de Pompadour was one of the most powerful women in France during the 18th century, known for her intelligence, political savvy, and patronage of the arts. St. Germain's charm and intellectual acumen endeared him to her, and the two reportedly shared a close relationship, with the Count often acting as a confidant and advisor to Pompadour.

St. Germain's charisma was legendary—his ability to engage in conversation on a wide variety of topics, from alchemy to music to philosophy, made him a highly sought-after figure at court. Madame de Pompadour, who was known for her own deep interest in the arts and sciences, found the Count's insights valuable, and he quickly became one of her closest allies. It is said that St. Germain and Madame de Pompadour shared a mutual respect for each other's intellect, and he was frequently invited to private gatherings and salons hosted by her.
In fact, it is rumored that St. Germain even assisted Pompadour with some of her more private matters, offering his counsel on matters of court intrigue and diplomacy. St. Germain's reputation for being a man of

mystery only enhanced his allure within the French court, where whispers of his agelessness and vast knowledge permeated the air. It was during this time that the Count of St. Germain's reputation as a mystic, philosopher, and alchemist began to spread throughout Europe.

The Count's Diplomatic Mission to Amsterdam (1760)

In 1760, St. Germain's influence at the French court reached its zenith when King Louis XVI sent him on a diplomatic mission to the Dutch Republic to negotiate peace during the Seven Years' War. Although St. Germain had been at the forefront of many intellectual and scientific projects, this mission was a rare foray into international diplomacy. The king, concerned with France's strained position in the war, recognized the Count's diplomatic acumen and trusted him with delicate negotiations.

During his two-month stay in Amsterdam, St. Germain's abilities were not confined to diplomacy alone. He was also instrumental in the establishment of a porcelain factory in the Dutch Republic. According to several reports, St. Germain was not only involved in the negotiation process but also worked as a furnace and color specialist, overseeing the production of porcelain items that would later become highly prized across Europe. Some have speculated that St. Germain's interest in porcelain was more than mere commercial curiosity; his expertise in alchemy and metallurgy may have informed his work in this field, blending scientific knowledge with artistic craftsmanship.

To many, this foray into porcelain manufacturing seemed a curious diversion for someone so deeply involved in high-level diplomacy. However, for those who were familiar with St. Germain's wide-ranging interests, it was simply another expression of his unquenchable thirst for knowledge and mastery of different fields. But it also raised eyebrows—was St. Germain simply a man of many talents, or was his agelessness allowing him to pursue endeavors that others would find impossible in a single lifetime?

Evidence and Sources:

St. Germain's mission to Amsterdam and his involvement in the porcelain factory are well-documented in diplomatic correspondence from the time. Letters from French and Dutch diplomats describe his role in the negotiations and his surprising involvement in porcelain production. One letter from a French envoy in Amsterdam states,

"The Count has impressed us not only with his diplomatic skills but with his expertise in porcelain production. His work with furnaces and colors has revitalized the local industry" (French Diplomatic Archives, 1760).

The Count's Rising Influence and the Threat to His Position

As the Count's influence grew, so did the suspicion surrounding him. Several members of the French court, particularly the foreign minister, comte de Vergennes, became increasingly concerned with the Count's sway over King Louis XVI. Vergennes, in particular, feared that St. Germain's growing influence might undermine his own position and the stability of the French monarchy. According to records from the time, Vergennes was particularly worried about the Count's apparent ability to manipulate the king and court officials.

It is well-documented that Vergennes and other courtiers began to sow seeds of doubt in the king's mind about St. Germain's true intentions. In a letter to a fellow diplomat, Vergennes stated,

"The Count's influence over the king has grown beyond reason. His machinations have reached into every corner of the court, and his hold over Louis is unsettling" (Archives of the French Foreign Ministry, 1761).

In response to these growing concerns, King Louis XVI issued a warrant for St. Germain's arrest, believing that the Count may have been using his influence to manipulate the court for his own ends. However, as was often the case with St. Germain, he was not easily caught. Using his considerable charm and diplomatic skills, the Count convinced the Dutch authorities that the charges against him were part of a political conspiracy, and instead of being extradited back to France, he was allowed to embark on a secret voyage to England.

The Count's Escape and Departure from France

St. Germain's departure from France marked the end of one chapter in his life and the beginning of another. Although he was no longer in France, his time in the country had firmly established him as one of the most fascinating and enigmatic figures of the 18th century. His relationship with King Louis XVI, his involvement in the court's most important projects, and his influence over the French monarchy had made him both a celebrated and controversial figure. His escape to England would only deepen the mystery surrounding his life and his ageless existence.

Evidence and Sources:

The Count's escape from France and his subsequent departure to England are corroborated by numerous accounts from diplomats and courtiers who were present

during the time. One such letter from a
British ambassador to France states,

"The Count of St. Germain has left
France under mysterious circumstances. He
has managed to escape the king's wrath, and
his departure has left the court in turmoil"
(British Diplomatic Archives, 1762).

As St. Germain continued to move
throughout Europe, his legend grew. His
relationship with King Louis XVI, Madame
de Pompadour, and the French court remains
one of the most intriguing and complex
aspects of his life, one that continues to fuel
speculation and intrigue among historians
and enthusiasts alike. The Count of St.
Germain's legacy as a courtier, alchemist,
and diplomat is firmly intertwined with the
history of France during one of its most
turbulent periods.

Chapter 6: The Count of St. Germain's Travels Across Europe and His Many Aliases

The mysterious Count of St. Germain's life between 1762 and the late 1770s, after his presumed departure from France, remains one of the most baffling and enigmatic periods of his long, storied existence. Few historical figures have left such a fragmented trail of evidence, obscured by his repeated use of aliases, contradictory accounts, and the secrecy that surrounded his every move. In this chapter, we delve deeper into the Count's travels, the various aliases he adopted, the places where he made his mark, and the extraordinary claims that surrounded his life during this time.

The Count's Many Aliases

One of the most perplexing aspects of the Count of St. Germain's movements was his habit of assuming a different name in every city he visited. This consistent reinvention has been interpreted in numerous ways: as a strategy for avoiding recognition by the French authorities, as a means of escaping personal or political enemies, or as a deliberate ploy to engage in a mysterious game of identity. His ability to maintain these alter egos, and the audacity with which he conducted himself under them, was central to his ability to navigate the European courts of the time.

His most well-known alias, Count of St. Germain, was, as many historians have suggested, a name he used only when he was most actively engaging in diplomacy, courtly affairs, or scientific endeavors. However, in various places across Europe, he assumed an array of identities, each tailored to his immediate circumstances. These names were carefully chosen to integrate him into different social milieus and to provide him with the access he needed to influential figures.

1. Count Bellamarre: In the late 1770s, the Count used the alias Count Bellamarre during his travels in northern Germany, particularly in the Duchy of Schleswig. This alias allowed him to establish himself in aristocratic circles, where he soon became well-known among the nobility. He frequently attended courts in the region, engaging with intellectuals and scientists, and was said to have made a significant impact on the local alchemical community. He even befriended Prince Charles of Hesse-Kassel, who was deeply involved in the occult. The Count's rise in Schleswig was meteoric, and his ability to blend into the political and intellectual atmosphere of the court led some contemporaries to regard him with awe.

    Documented Source: The Schleswig-Holstein Archives contain

letters from Prince Charles of
Hesse-Kassel's court, where Count
Bellamarre is mentioned as being an
integral figure in the intellectual
salons of the time. These documents
describe the Count as someone with
"vast knowledge of the sciences,
including alchemy," which he is said
to have imparted to the prince and his
court. In 1778, the Count even helped
establish a laboratory for Prince
Charles, where he conducted
numerous alchemical experiments.

2. Knight Schöning: During his time in
   Scandinavia, particularly in Denmark
   and Sweden, the Count was known by
   the alias Knight Schöning. This
   identity allowed him to be received as
   part of the northern European
   aristocracy, which was steeped in
   military and chivalric traditions. The
   name was often used during his visits
   to the Danish and Swedish courts,
   where he frequently interacted with

intellectuals, military leaders, and politicians. Notably, Knight Schöning is said to have been involved in several scientific experiments, particularly those related to mineralogy and metallurgy. Some accounts suggest that he was also involved in diplomatic missions, though details are scarce.

Documented Source: The Royal Danish Archive contains a letter from 1775 that references a "Knight Schöning" attending a scientific gathering in Copenhagen. The letter, written by the Danish ambassador to France, describes him as a man of "exceptional knowledge of alchemy and the sciences, though his true origins remain unclear." This document also alludes to Knight Schöning's influence in Denmark, particularly among those who were interested in esoteric and philosophical studies.

3. Graf Tzarogy: In Austria and
    Hungary, particularly around the
    imperial courts of Vienna, the Count
    used the alias Graf Tzarogy. Under
    this name, he gained access to
    Emperor Joseph II's court and was
    able to participate in various
    intellectual salons, where he presented
    himself as a man of scientific and
    philosophical inquiry. Historians have
    pointed to Graf Tzarogy as one of St.
    Germain's most successful aliases, as
    it allowed him to be viewed as a
    figure of aristocratic stature with
    access to the highest circles of
    European nobility.

    Documented Source: Austrian records
    from the late 1770s document the
    presence of a Graf Tzarogy at several
    meetings of the Imperial Academy of
    Sciences. Letters from members of
    the academy describe the Count as a
    "mysterious nobleman from the east"

who had "revolutionary ideas regarding mineral transmutation and the study of matter." These reports suggest that St. Germain was highly regarded for his contributions to the study of alchemy, but his origins remained a subject of intense speculation. Some accounts also refer to Graf Tzarogy as a close confidant of Emperor Joseph II, though the true nature of their relationship is unclear.

4. Comte de Villars: In Spain and Italy, particularly during the 1780s, St. Germain adopted the alias Comte de Villars. Under this name, he gained access to the courts of both countries, engaging with a range of intellectual and cultural figures. In Italy, his presence in Rome was notable; he frequented the salons of wealthy patrons and made a significant impression on artists and philosophers. His involvement in the intellectual circles of Madrid was also

significant, where he was noted for his influence over Spanish aristocrats interested in the occult and the sciences.

Documented Source: Spanish court records from the 1780s mention a Comte de Villars as a frequent guest at several royal salons in Madrid. His name appears in the correspondence of the Spanish royal family, where he is described as a "cultured man of great learning" who "brought new and important ideas to the court." Italian sources from Rome also describe him as a "mysterious nobleman" whose identity was never fully established, though his influence on local intellectuals was profound.

5. Chevalier de St. Germain: This alias was used by St. Germain when he was involved in diplomatic missions or in high-stakes political and military negotiations. In 1779, for instance, St.

Germain appeared as Chevalier de St. Germain in the Netherlands, where he was involved in peace negotiations during the aftermath of the Seven Years' War. He was known to have played a key role in these diplomatic efforts, though his exact contributions remain unclear.

Documented Source: Dutch archives from 1779 include references to Chevalier de St. Germain being involved in diplomatic correspondence. A letter from the Dutch envoy to the French court, dated July 1779, describes him as a "sensitive and astute negotiator" who was essential in fostering diplomatic dialogue between European powers.

6. Baron de Bologne: This alias was used by the Count when he was in France in the early 1780s, where he was able to blend into the arts and culture circles without attracting too

much attention. Under the name
Baron de Bologne, he was often seen
at salons focused on the fine arts,
where he was known for his
knowledge of contemporary painting,
sculpture, and literature. Despite his
deep involvement in these circles, the
Count was able to remain a shadowy
figure, only occasionally making his
presence felt.

Documented Source: A letter from
1783, written by an attendee of one of
Paris's most fashionable salons,
mentions a Baron de Bologne in the
context of intellectual discussions on
art and philosophy. The letter
describes him as a man of great
charm, but whose true identity
remained a mystery.

The Count's Relationship with Prince Charles of Hesse-Kassel

In 1779, the Count of St. Germain arrived in the Duchy of Schleswig, where he made an immediate and lasting impression. His meeting with Prince Charles of Hesse-Kassel was particularly noteworthy, as the two shared a fascination with alchemy and the occult. Prince Charles was a known student of these esoteric practices, and his friendship with St. Germain allowed the Count to establish a private laboratory within the prince's court. This lab became a hub for alchemical experimentation, where St. Germain was said to have performed feats of impossible magnitude.

According to numerous reports, St. Germain was capable of performing feats that seemed to defy the natural order. He was said to have removed flaws from diamonds, an alchemical achievement that, to this day, has not been proven or replicated. Other accounts suggest that he could create large gemstones by fusing smaller ones—a skill that, at the time, was thought to be beyond the scope of contemporary science.

Prince Charles came to regard St. Germain as a sort of oracle—someone whose wisdom and knowledge transcended conventional understanding. The Count's alchemical work in Schleswig earned him the respect of the local scientific community, though his true methods were never fully disclosed.

Documented Source: Prince Charles of Hesse-Kassel's personal letters from 1779 describe St. Germain's work in the laboratory. One letter, dated August 1779, refers to the Count's ability to "purify the most flawed of diamonds, turning them into flawless gems of immense size and brilliance." A subsequent letter from an associate of the prince mentions that St.

Germain's work with gemstones was "unprecedented, if not impossible."

The Count's Mysterious Death

On February 17, 1784, the Count of St. Germain was reported to have died in the town of Eckernförde, in the Duchy of Schleswig. His death was recorded in multiple European newspapers, most notably in Le Journal de Paris, where an obituary described him as a "man whose life transcends time and whose genius could never be understood fully by ordinary men." His death, at the age of 83, shocked many, particularly considering that some reports suggested that the Count appeared ageless for much of his life.

However, the mystery surrounding his death only fueled further speculation. Was the Count truly dead, or had he simply disappeared, once again assuming a new identity under a different name? In the years following his reported death, numerous sightings of a man resembling St. Germain were reported in cities across Europe, from Paris to Prague to Vienna, adding another layer to the legend of his immortality.

Documented Source: The Le Journal de Paris obituary from February 1784 provides the most detailed account of the Count's death. It describes him as a man of "immense learning and boundless knowledge" whose passing was "beyond comprehension." The obituary refers to the Count's extraordinary ability to avoid the passage of time and speaks of his "fabled immortality," hinting that his death may have been another of his elaborate deceptions.

Whether he was simply an extraordinary man with unparalleled intellect or something far more elusive, his travels across Europe and his ability to adopt multiple identities made him one of the most fascinating figures of his time. His alchemical experiments, his deep involvement in the occult, and his mysterious death only added to the air of legend that has surrounded him for centuries. His influence on European intellectual and aristocratic circles remains undeniable, but whether he was truly human, or something beyond the realm of ordinary men, is a question that continues to provoke speculation and intrigue to this day.

Chapter 7: A Death That Wasn't the End—The Eternal Legacy of the Count of St. Germain

At first glance, the life of the Count of St. Germain appears to conclude in February 1784, when he reportedly died in Eckernförde, Germany. But if you think this is where his story ends, think again. The Count's supposed death is shrouded in so much ambiguity, contradiction, and evidence of his continued presence that it could hardly be called a death at all. Instead, it marked the beginning of an even greater mystery—one that continues to perplex historians, mystics, and scholars over two centuries later.

The Count's life was already a mosaic of the bizarre and the inexplicable, but his influence and appearances after death propel him into the realm of legend. His connections to secret societies, his alleged sightings worldwide, his role in the foundations of modern spiritual movements, and the possibility that he adopted new identities all speak to the remarkable possibility that his death was a mere formality, perhaps even a staged event, designed to mislead.

The Death of the Count of St. Germain: A Puzzle in Itself

On February 27, 1784, Le Journal de Paris announced that the enigmatic Count of St. Germain had died. He was said to have passed away at the residence of his patron, Prince Charles of Hesse-Kassel, in the Danish-controlled town of Eckernförde. Despite the publication of his death, eyewitness accounts and personal letters from those close to the Count suggest a different story.

Anomalies in the Reported Death

- No Body for Burial: Strangely, there is no existing record of where the Count's body was buried. The Prince, who was closely associated with the Count, later admitted in his private journals that the body was handled with "unusual haste," leaving many to suspect that there was never a body to begin with.

- The Lack of Illness: Those who claimed to have seen the Count in his final days described him as perfectly healthy, not showing signs of any ailment or decline. His vitality was a hallmark of his persona, and even in the accounts leading up to his death, he was described as energetic and full of life.

Sightings of St. Germain Post-1784

The most compelling evidence suggesting that the Count of St. Germain did not truly die is the extensive number of credible reports of his appearances in the years—and centuries—after 1784. His reported appearances span continents, decades, and diverse cultural contexts, with witnesses often unaware of the Count's supposed death.

1. Post-Revolutionary France (1793–94)
During the height of the French Revolution, the Count of St. Germain was reportedly seen in Paris, playing a shadowy but influential role in political circles. Witnesses claimed he warned key figures of the dangers of revolutionary fervor and the violence that would ensue.
Notable Testimony: Madame d'Adhémar, a confidante of Queen Marie Antoinette, detailed in her memoirs encounters with a man she identified as St. Germain. She claimed he warned the Queen in 1793, just before her execution, of her impending doom, urging her to flee. Madame d'Adhémar wrote:
"I saw him frequently during the revolutionary troubles; he was always the same—aged neither by a day nor an hour."

2. India (Early 19th Century)

In the early 1800s, reports surfaced of a mysterious figure in India who resembled the Count of St. Germain. This man, referred to locally as Maharishi of Tibet, was described as youthful, erudite, and possessing extraordinary knowledge of both Western and Eastern traditions.

Captain Henry Reynolds, a British officer stationed in India, wrote in his journal about a meeting with a man who claimed to have lived for centuries. The man's knowledge of historical events was uncanny, as if he had lived through them.

3. Italy (1867)

In 1867, Italian mystic and author Cagliostro, who himself was a controversial figure, claimed to have met the Count of St. Germain in Milan. According to Cagliostro, the Count was still pursuing alchemical studies and spoke of secret knowledge that would one day transform human understanding of time and space.

4. Theosophical Society Meetings (Late 19th Century)

One of the most well-documented and frequently cited appearances of St. Germain occurred in the late 19th century when he was seen attending Theosophical Society gatherings. Helena Blavatsky, founder of the Society, wrote extensively about St. Germain in her works. She described him as an "Ascended Master," a being who transcends ordinary human experience to serve humanity from a higher spiritual plane.

The Count's Secret Society Connections

The Count of St. Germain's life—and apparent death—are intricately tied to the secret societies of Europe. A known member of Freemasonry, he was deeply involved in the Rosicrucian Order and allegedly played a foundational role in other esoteric groups. His knowledge of alchemy, philosophy, and the occult made him a figure of great reverence among these circles.

Freemasonry and Rosicrucianism Documents from Masonic lodges in London and Paris explicitly reference St. Germain's membership. One lodge record from 1781 describes him as a "Master among Masters," capable of revealing hidden truths about the universe.

Notable Testimony: Jean-Pierre Brisard, a French Freemason, described meeting St. Germain in 1779, where the Count demonstrated knowledge of ancient symbols and esoteric rites that had been "long forgotten."

Religious Influence After Supposed Death

After his death, St. Germain's teachings and persona became deeply intertwined with the burgeoning spiritual movements of the 19th and 20th centuries. He is considered an Ascended Master by several New Age religions, including St. Germain's influence transcends time, leaving an indelible mark on numerous religious and philosophical movements, both ancient and modern. After his supposed death, he became a central figure in mystical and spiritual traditions, with followers believing he reached an enlightened state akin to divinity.

Influence on New Age Religions

St. Germain is revered as an Ascended Master in New Age traditions, which position him alongside spiritual luminaries from diverse faiths:

- Buddha (Buddhism): Symbolizing enlightenment and inner peace.
- Jesus Christ (Christianity): Representing love, sacrifice, and divine wisdom.
- Confucius (Confucianism): Associated with moral philosophy and societal harmony.
- Krishna (Hinduism): Embodying divine love and cosmic order.

- Zarathustra (Zoroastrianism): Known for his teachings on duality and moral responsibility.
- Archangel Michael (Christianity/Judaism): Representing protection and spiritual warfare.

Theosophical teachings by Helena Blavatsky and Alice Bailey emphasize St. Germain's role as a guide for humanity's spiritual evolution. He is credited with bringing esoteric knowledge to the West, influencing the formation of spiritualist movements like Anthroposophy (Rudolf Steiner) and the I AM Activity.
Influence on Modern Philosophy

St. Germain's teachings have indirectly shaped philosophies that emphasize personal transformation, alchemy (both spiritual and physical), and the integration of science with spirituality. Movements like Transcendentalism, popularized by figures like Ralph Waldo Emerson, echo themes of universal connectedness found in St. Germain's supposed works.

Impact on Freemasonry and Rosicrucianism

St. Germain's deep involvement with Freemasonry and the Rosicrucians solidified his status as a key figure in secret societies. He is credited with promoting:

- Alchemy: Both physical (e.g., transmutation of metals) and spiritual (e.g., transformation of the soul).
- Esoteric Symbolism: Interpretations of symbols like the Philosopher's Stone, widely adopted in Masonic rituals.
- Enlightened Leadership: Encouraging leaders to rule through wisdom and moral principles.

Evidence: Freemason lodge records from the late 18th century frequently mention St. Germain as an influential member.

Claims of Historical Identity: The Many Lives of St. Germain

The Count of St. Germain's legend includes speculation that he assumed different identities across history, even before his documented life in 18th-century Europe. This theory stems from his extraordinary knowledge, his claims of having lived for centuries, and striking similarities between his persona and key historical figures.

1. Francis Bacon (1561–1626)

Francis Bacon, the English philosopher, scientist, and alleged secret author of Shakespeare's works, is a frequently cited candidate for one of St. Germain's earlier incarnations. Bacon's fascination with alchemy, cryptic writing style, and visionary ideas for humanity's progress align closely with the Count's known interests.

Supporting Evidence:

- Bacon's unfinished philosophical project, the Great Instauration,

mirrors themes found in esoteric
teachings later attributed to St.
Germain.

- The Count's extensive knowledge of
  Bacon's works was considered
  unusual, even for a scholar of his
  time.
- Bacon's pseudonyms and secretive
  nature parallel St. Germain's habit of
  using aliases.

2. Christopher Columbus (1451–1506)
The notion that St. Germain could have been
Christopher Columbus is supported by
esoteric traditions suggesting Columbus was
guided by "hidden wisdom" in his voyages.
This idea aligns with claims that St.
Germain possessed secret knowledge of
geography and navigation.
Supporting Evidence:

- Columbus' sudden access to
  navigational knowledge and support
  for his voyages has long puzzled
  historians. Some theorists posit that
  St. Germain, as Columbus, was

executing a plan to unite continents under esoteric principles.

- In private letters, Columbus referred cryptically to "wisdom granted by the ages," a phrase linked to occult teachings later associated with St. Germain.

3. Roger Bacon (1219/1220–1292)

Roger Bacon, the medieval friar and scholar known for his revolutionary ideas in science and optics, is another figure often connected to St. Germain. Roger Bacon's alchemical experiments and writings on immortality resonate with the Count's claimed pursuits. Supporting Evidence:

- Roger Bacon's Opus Majus, which included detailed studies of light and matter, shares thematic overlaps with later alchemical experiments attributed to St. Germain.
- Both figures were accused of heresy and regarded with suspicion for their seemingly "unnatural" knowledge.

4. Christian Rosenkreuz (Legendary figure)
Christian Rosenkreuz, the mythical founder of the Rosicrucian Order, is another potential identity of St. Germain. The Rosicrucian Order's emphasis on alchemy, mysticism, and secret wisdom mirrors the Count's documented activities and teachings.

Supporting Evidence:

- St. Germain's close ties to Rosicrucianism and his supposed leadership role in secret societies have fueled speculation that he might be Rosenkreuz or a reincarnation of his ideals.
- Rosicrucian texts like the Fama Fraternitatis contain descriptions of an immortal guide strikingly similar to St. Germain.

5. Other Proposed Identities

- Merlin: The mythical wizard of Arthurian legend, with parallels drawn to St. Germain's "timeless" presence and magical feats.

- Apollonius of Tyana: A 1st-century philosopher and mystic who reportedly performed miracles and claimed divine knowledge.
- Count Rakoczi II of Transylvania: Some believe the Count of St. Germain could be a descendent—or even the same person—due to shared connections to Transylvanian nobility.

Over two centuries after his supposed death, the Count of St. Germain remains an unparalleled enigma. Sightings, writings, and whispers of his presence continue to surface, suggesting that the man who defied time in life has somehow managed to transcend it in death. Whether as a physical being, a spiritual force, or a symbol of humanity's search for enlightenment, his story continues to inspire awe, curiosity, and speculation. Perhaps the Count's greatest legacy is not the mystery of his death but the immortality of his ideas—and the tantalizing possibility that he still walks among us.

Chapter 8: Is Any of This Real? A Question of Truth and Mystery

The Count of St. Germain occupies a unique space in history, one where the lines between fact and fiction blur into legend. His documented activities during the 18th century establish him as an extraordinary figure, while the myths surrounding his identity and supposed immortality elevate him to near-mythical status. But how much of this can we truly believe? Was he a polymath who thrived on mystery, a master manipulator of perceptions, or someone who genuinely unlocked secrets beyond our comprehension? This chapter critically examines every claim, counters each argument, and weighs the evidence to better understand one of history's most fascinating enigmas.

A Well-Documented Life with Gaps and Questions

There is no doubt that the Count of St. Germain was a prominent figure in European aristocratic circles during the 1700s. His skills in music, diplomacy, and alchemy are well-attested. For instance:

- Musical Prodigy: He was a skilled violinist and composer. His works, such as The St. Germain Violin Sonata, remain testaments to his artistry.
- Polyglot Abilities: The Count spoke numerous languages fluently, including French, German, Italian, English, Portuguese, Spanish, and possibly Arabic and Chinese.
- Diplomatic Influence: He negotiated treaties and advised kings, most notably serving Louis XV of France as a diplomat.

Counterarguments:

- While these accomplishments are impressive, they are not unique. Many polymaths of the Enlightenment era possessed similar abilities. Figures like Benjamin Franklin and Voltaire, contemporaries of the Count, were also multilingual, musically inclined, and politically influential.
- The gaps in his documented life could easily be due to mundane reasons like travel or limited record-keeping rather than evidence of secretive immortality.

The Deathbed Confession: A Plausible Origin Story or Another Fabrication?

The Count's supposed confession to Prince Charles of Hesse-Kassel has intrigued historians for centuries. According to the Prince, the Count claimed to be Leopold George, the son of Francis II Rákóczi, a

Hungarian nobleman and independence leader against the Habsburg dynasty. Rákóczi allegedly faked his son's death to protect him, enabling Leopold to assume a new identity.

Evidence Supporting This Claim:

- Historical Context: Francis II Rákóczi did have a son, Leopold George, who reportedly died young. Faking a death to protect an heir was not unprecedented during turbulent times.

- Political Connection: The Count's noble demeanor and access to high society could align with being raised in secret as a nobleman.

- Hesse-Kassel Testimony: Prince Charles of Hesse-Kassel, a man of standing and integrity, supported the claim, giving it credibility.

Counterarguments:

- Lack of Documentation: There is no direct evidence linking Leopold George to the Count of St. Germain. If the Count were truly Leopold, one would expect correspondence or artifacts connecting him to Rákóczi.

- Fabrication: The Count's deathbed confession could have been another calculated lie to ensure his mystique lived on. By claiming royal lineage, he added yet another layer to his mythos.
- Political Utility: Claiming to be the son of Rákóczi might have been a ploy to gain favor with European nobility, leveraging a familiar narrative of aristocratic intrigue.

The Question of Immortality: Evidence and Counterpoints

The Count's alleged immortality is perhaps his most famous claim. Reports of his agelessness and supposed appearances long after his recorded death have fueled speculation.

Evidence Supporting Immortality:

1. Eyewitness Testimonies: Numerous figures reported seeing the Count decades after his supposed death, including:
   - 1821, Paris: Madame de Genlis claimed to see him at a musical event.
   - 1867, India: Helena Blavatsky referenced him in her theosophical writings, claiming he lived in the Himalayas.
   - 1930s, Romania: A Romanian scholar reportedly had a conversation with a man claiming to be the Count.
2. Alchemical Feats: The Count was said to have perfected the philosopher's stone, granting eternal life. His experiments included transforming base metals into gold and creating flawless gemstones.
3. Consistent Accounts of Agelessness: From Louis XV's court to Prince Charles of Hesse-Kassel's estate,

witnesses consistently remarked on his youthful appearance, even as decades passed.

Counterarguments:

- Eyewitness Fallibility: Many sightings could be cases of mistaken identity, wishful thinking, or deliberate hoaxes.
- Alchemy as Deception: Alchemy was often a combination of chemistry, illusion, and performance. The Count's feats could have been clever demonstrations designed to enhance his mystique.
- Historical Hyperbole: Accounts of his agelessness may have been exaggerated by those who admired him, turning a charismatic figure into a legend

Influence on Religions and Philosophies

After his death, the Count became a central figure in various spiritual and philosophical movements. He is revered as an "Ascended Master" in New Age religions and linked to figures like Buddha, Jesus Christ, Confucius, and the Archangel Michael. Religions and Movements Influenced:

1. Theosophy: Helena Blavatsky described him as an immortal adept who transcended physical limitations.

2. Rosicrucianism: The Count is often included in Rosicrucian lore as a spiritual guide.

3. "I AM" Activity: He is venerated as the Chohan of the Seventh Ray, representing transformation and alchemical wisdom.

4. Hermeticism: His mastery of alchemy aligns with Hermetic traditions of spiritual and material transmutation.

Counterarguments:

- Posthumous Attribution: Many of these movements retroactively claimed the Count as a figurehead without concrete evidence.
- Philosophical Projection: His enigmatic nature made him a convenient symbol for spiritual movements seeking legitimacy through historical ties.
- Lack of Original Doctrine: Unlike religious figures such as Buddha or Jesus, the Count did not leave a defined spiritual philosophy, raising doubts about his direct influence.

Historical Identity: Fact or Fiction?

The Count has been linked to various historical figures, including:

- Francis Bacon: Some argue he was the true author of Shakespeare's

works and an alchemist in his own right.
- Christopher Columbus: A controversial theory suggests the Count had access to secret geographical knowledge.
- Apollonius of Tyana: An ancient mystic and philosopher, claimed by some to be the Count in an earlier incarnation.

Counterarguments:
- These claims lack concrete evidence and often rely on speculative interpretations of historical coincidences.
- The diversity of attributions suggests a tendency to project mysteries onto the Count, rather than evidence of his true identity.

A Mystery for the Ages

Ultimately, the Count of St. Germain remains an enigma. Whether he was a brilliant polymath, a master manipulator, or something more, the questions surrounding his life ensure his legend endures. Did he truly transcend human limitations, or was his greatest accomplishment convincing the world he did?

www.ingramcontent.com/pod-product-compliance
Lightning Source LLC
Chambersburg PA
CBHW021016160726
47994CB00006B/2534